How You Can Know The Will Of God

by Kenneth E. Hagin

Second Edition
Tenth Printing • 1980

In the United States write:
Kenneth Hagin Ministries, Inc.
P.O. Box 50126
Tulsa, Oklahoma 74150

In Canada write:
Kenneth Hagin Ministries
P.O. Box 335
Islington (Toronto), Ontario
Canada, M9A 4X3

ISBN #0-89276-019-2

CONTENTS

1

THE INNER MAN—THE REAL YOU

For as many as are led by the Spirit of God, they are the sons of God.
                                                    —Romans 8:14

The Spirit itself beareth witness with our spirit, that we are the children of God.
                                                    —Romans 8:16

The spirit of man is the candle of the Lord, searching all the inward parts of the belly.
                                                    —Proverbs 20:27

T HE WRITER of the book of Proverbs said that the spirit of man is the candle (lamp) of the Lord. That means that God will enlighten and guide us through our spirits.

Too often, however, we seek guidance every other way except the way that God said it was going to come. We judge by our physical senses, but nowhere does God say He will guide us by our senses. Or we often look at things from a mental standpoint. But God said *"the spirit of man is the candle of the Lord,"* which means that He will guide us through our spirits.

Man is a spirit being. He has a soul, and he lives in a physical body. But he is a spirit being because he is made in the likeness of God. Jesus said that God is a Spirit.

When the body is dead and in the grave, man lives on. Paul, speaking of physical death, said, *"For I am in a strait betwixt two, having a desire to depart, and to be with Christ; which is far better"* (Phil. 1:23). To show that he was talking about physical death, he then said, *"Nevertheless to abide in the flesh is more needful for you"* (v. 24). He was saying, "When I depart I am going to be with the Lord."

Who was Paul talking about when he said "I"? He was not talking about his body, for his body wasn't going to depart. We will have a new body one day and it will be raised, but *"the inward man is renewed day by day"* (2 Cor. 4:16).

You see, there is an outward man and an inward man. The outward man is not the real you. The outward man is only the "house" (body) you live in. *The inward man is the real you.*

Before we can understand how God will guide us through our spirits, we must first find out what our spirit is. This inward man—or as he is called by Peter, *"the hidden man of the heart"* (1 Peter 3:4)—is the spirit of man. When the Bible speaks of the heart, it is speaking of the spirit, the inward man, or the hidden man. This is the real man. When Paul says, *"Therefore if any man be in Christ, he is a new creature . . . ."* (2 Cor. 5:17), he is talking about the inward man, the real man. You certainly didn't get a new body when you were born again but the real you became a new man in Christ. Another translation says, "Therefore if any man be in Christ, there is a new self."

Often our terms are so indistinct in describing things that they are confusing. It would be better to say things as the Bible says them. For instance, in First Thessalonians 5:23, Paul prays for the church at Thessalonica, saying, *"I pray God your whole spirit and soul and body be preserved blameless unto the coming of our Lord Jesus Christ."* Paul begins with the inside and comes to the outside. He begins with the inward man and comes to the outward man. Usually people misquote that and put the body first instead of the spirit, because they are more body-conscious than spirit-conscious. We need to reverse the order and become more spirit-conscious.

We will not be able to get what God is saying to us in our spirit, and spiritual things will be indistinct to us until we become spirit-conscious. The more spirit-conscious we become, the more real the leading of the Lord will be to us.

We need to think of ourselves as spirit beings, possessing souls, and living in bodies. Our thinking has been so wrong on this for years that we have confused the whole issue.

Some of the leading Bible scholars in our land seem startled when I ask, "What is the difference between the spirit of man and the soul of man?" They say, "Well, I have always thought they were the same." Many times preachers use the terms interchangeably, leaving the impression that the spirit and the soul are the same. But they are not. *"For the word of God is quick, and powerful, and sharper than any twoedged sword, piercing even to the dividing asunder of **soul and spirit** . . . ."* (Heb. 4:12).

6

Paul said, "For if I pray in an unknown tongue, my **spirit** prayeth, but my **understanding** is unfruitful" (1 Cor. 14:14). Our understanding is a part of our soul. Paul said, "My understanding is unfruitful. I didn't pray out of my soul (intellect or mind). That wasn't my soul praying." He said, "If I pray in an unknown tongue, my spirit prayeth."

I especially like the expression used in Proverbs 20:27, "The spirit of man is the candle of the Lord, searching all the inward parts of the belly." Jesus said, "If any man thirst, let him come unto me, and drink. He that believeth on me, as the scripture hath said, out of his belly shall flow rivers of living water. (But this spake he of the Spirit, which they that believe on him should receive: for the Holy Ghost was not yet given; because that Jesus was not yet glorified)" (John 7:37-39). As a result of receiving the Holy Spirit, out of the "belly" shall flow rivers of living water. Another translation says, "Out of his innermost being shall flow rivers of living water."

The Amplified translation of First Corinthians 14:14 says, "For if I pray in an (unknown) tongue, **my spirit** (by the Holy Spirit within me) prays." When you pray in tongues, it comes out of your innermost being, your spirit. Therefore, when we read, "The spirit of man is the candle of the Lord, searching all the inward parts of the belly," we see that the spirit of man is our innermost being—the real man (or woman).

A man's *spirit*—the innermost man, the real man—receives eternal life and is *born again*. But his intellect and emotions, which compose *the soul*, still have to be dealt with. They are not born again; they are *renewed*.

Paul speaks about the renewing of the mind in Romans 12:2, "And be not conformed to this world: but be ye transformed by the renewing of your mind . . . . " This is a process. (The epistle of James was written to Christians. Yet in the first chapter he said, "Receive with meekness the engrafted word, which is able to save your souls.")

Jesus said, "That which is born of the Spirit is spirit" (John 3:6). It is our spirit that is born again. Our soul can be renewed or restored by the Word of God.

With our spirit we contact the spiritual world; with our soul we contact the mental world; and with our body we

contact the physical world.

Sometimes we hear people talk about "dying out to self." However, we don't want to die out to self; we want to crucify the flesh. This isn't something that God does for you; you must do it yourself.

Paul said, *"I beseech you therefore, brethren, by the mercies of God, that ye present your bodies a living sacrifice, holy, acceptable unto God, which is your reasonable service"* (Rom. 12:1). He didn't tell you to "die out to self or the flesh," but he did tell you to do something with the flesh.

Paul said in Romans 6:13, *"Neither yield ye your members as instruments of unrighteousness unto sin . . . ."* After you are born again, your body is going to want to keep on doing the same things it always has done, but Paul said not to let it. The man on the inside, the inward man, has become a new man in Christ. Let this inward man dominate the outward man.

The reason many people have had a mistaken concept of soul and spirit is that they don't thoroughly understand the new birth. We are more than justified. We have become a new man; a new creature in Christ.

This man on the inside—which is the spirit of man through whom God will deal—has become a new man. The old things that were in this old man are gone now. Spiritual death was in there. The nature of the devil was in there. Hatred and lying were in there. But now the love of God is in there. Now the nature of God is in there. This is the man who is to be the dominant one. We are to listen to him, because it is through this man—through our spirits—that God will guide us.

2

GUIDANCE THROUGH THE INNER MAN

THE INWARD man we discussed in Chapter 1 has a "voice" which we call conscience, intuition, inner guidance, or the inward witness.

There has been much discussion as to whether the conscience is a safe guide. However, if your spirit has become a new man in Christ, with the life and nature of God in it, then your conscience is a safe guide, because *your conscience is the voice of your spirit*. That is how God guides you.

Of course, a person who has never been born again could not follow the voice of his spirit. His spirit would be unregenerate. His conscience would permit him to do anything. But when you have the nature and life of God in you, your conscience won't permit you to do just anything.

If you are a born-again Christian, the Holy Spirit is living and abiding in your spirit. He does not communicate directly with your mind, because *He is not in your mind; He is in your spirit*. He communicates with you through your spirit.

Jesus said, *"We* (my Father and I) *will come unto him, and make our abode with him"* (John 14:23). Paul said, *"Know ye not that ye are the temple of God, and that the Spirit of God dwelleth in you?"* (1 Cor. 3:16). Again, writing to the Corinthians in the second letter, he said, *"Ye are the temple of the living God; as God hath said, I will dwell in them, and walk in them; and I will be their God, and they shall be my people"* (2 Cor. 6:16). Therefore, if God is dwelling in us, then that is where He is going to speak to us.

It is your spirit, not the Holy Spirit, that condemns you if you do wrong as a Christian. The Holy Spirit does not convict of sin. Jesus said the only sin the Holy Spirit will convict the world of is the sin of rejecting Jesus. It is your own spirit that knows the very moment you have done wrong.

Shortly after I was born again, healed by the power of God, and back in high school, a boy asked me a question. I had been around some boys who, although they didn't actually curse, used some words that were almost that. Evidently I had picked up one of those words. When the boy asked me a question, I answered, "Well, it's none of your darn business."

The minute I said it, on the inside of me I knew I had done wrong, and I asked God's forgiveness right then and there. I apologized to the boy and said, "I want you to forgive me for talking like that." He hadn't thought a thing about it, but I knew it was no way for Christians to talk. It was my spirit, not the Holy Spirit, that convicted me, because my spirit has the nature and the life of God in it.

Paul says some illuminating things about his conscience. For example, he said he always obeyed his conscience. Notice in Romans 8:16, Paul said, *"The Spirit itself beareth witness with our spirit, that we are the children of God."* Too many times people think that this witness he is talking about is a physical something. It isn't. The Bible does not say the Spirit bears witness with our bodies.

Feeling is the voice of the *body.*

Reason is the voice of the *soul, or mind.*

Conscience is the voice of the *spirit.*

If we go by feelings, we are going to be in trouble.

People say, "I just felt like the Lord heard me." It makes no difference whether you felt like it or not; if the Word of God states it, it is true. If God said He heard and answered your prayer, He did.

Base your faith on the Word; not on your feelings. This verse does not say that the Spirit bears witness with our *bodies* or with our *feelings.* It says, *"The Spirit itself beareth witness with our spirit."* The Word and the Spirit agree. The Spirit will take this Word and witness to your heart.

Jesus said, *"When he, the Spirit of truth, is come . . . he shall receive of mine, and shall shew it unto you"* (John 16:13,14). He said to His disciples, *"He shall teach you all things, and bring all things to your remembrance, whatsoever I have said unto you"* (John 14:26). He also said, *"He will show you things to come"* (John 16:13). He bears witness with your spirit. Then He leads you. Romans 8:14 says, *"For as many as are led by the Spirit of God, they are the sons of God."*

It is not for us to tell the Lord how to lead us. In the Acts of the Apostles and elsewhere in the Bible we see how at times some received guidance through a vision. We read where others received guidance from an angel who appeared and told them certain things. Too many times we seek guidance in that way instead of listening to what the Bible says. However, such phenomena didn't happen every day in these people's lives, either. They occurred once or twice in the entire lifetime of some of them. Too many times when God is trying to bear witness with our spirits—trying to guide us—we won't listen because we want something dramatic, like a vision or an angel.

For guidance some people put out what they call a "fleece" before the Lord. I tried that one time back in 1941. I put out a fleece; I followed my fleece; and I got fleeced! That cured me.

The New Testament does not say, "As many as are led by fleeces, they are the sons of God." Of course, Gideon did put out a fleece. But we are not living in the day he lived in. We are not living under the covenant he lived under. We have a New Covenant, established on better promises.

It doesn't say anywhere in the New Testament that Peter, Paul, or any of the apostles ever told the people to put out a fleece before the Lord. In fact, this practice is really dangerous, for we put the fleece out in this sense world, in the area where Satan is god (2 Cor. 4:4).

Once when I tried out for the pastorate of a church in Texas, I put out a fleece before the Lord that if the congregation voted 100 percent for me to come as their new pastor, I would accept this as the Lord's will and go. I got every vote and accepted the pastorate. But, as I said, I got fleeced!

That was the most miserable time I ever spent in my life. I lost all anointing to preach. While preparing my sermons, I would feel as if a fire was in my bones, but the minute I stepped inside the church door for services, it was as if someone had poured a bucket of cold water on me.

I was out of the will of God. I was only in His permissive will, and things don't work right when you are only in the permissive will of God. It's like washing your feet with your socks on.

That was the only time I ever missed it in taking a church. In other churches, I didn't put out a fleece. I didn't get every vote that was cast. But I knew on the inside of me, by that inward witness and by that inward voice, what I was to do, and I did it.

Sometimes folks don't want to take the responsibility themselves, yet that is where the responsibility is. It is a lot easier to put it off on the Lord and say, "Lord, if You want me to do that, then You open the door. If You don't, then You shut it." It is easier to do that than to wait on God until you know the answer on the inside of you. And sometimes it takes times of waiting to hear this inward witness.

We get so busy physically and mentally that spiritual things become indistinct to us. It is easier to get quiet with your body than to get quiet with your mind. You can make just as much noise with your mind as you can with your hands and feet! Sometimes when you try to sleep, though your body is relaxed, your mind is still noisy. It is still churning with the day's activities, ideas, and plans, or worries and anxieties about the future.

Here is an area where praying in tongues is a great advantage. *"For if I pray in an unknown tongue, my spirit prayeth, but my understandng is unfruitful"* (1 Cor. 14:14).

While praying, has your mind ever wandered to other things? It used to take me an hour sometimes to get my mind quiet, but now I have found that the best way is to pray in other tongues. When you pray in other tongues, your mind grows quiet. Once it is quiet, you become more conscious of your own spirit and of spiritual things. When praying in other tongues and worshipping God, your spirit is in direct contact with God, who is a Spirit and the Father of spirits. Because your mind is not active, your prayer language doesn't come out of your head but out of your heart.

If we would train our spirits, we would know inside with a "yes" or a "no" just what to do in every area of life; even in minor things. We spend practically our entire lifetime in the mental and physical realms. We've developed our head a lot of times at the expense of our heart. The knowledge of our intellect has taken the throne in our life, and our spirit, which should guide us, is kept locked away in prison, so to speak, and is not permitted to function.

That inward witness is seeking to give guidance to our mind. We all know that there are a thousand and one things we would never have done if we had listened to that inward witness.

We would not have invested and lost money in certain ventures; we would never have chosen certain persons as our companions. (I'm not referring just to marriage partners, but to certain people with whom we get involved.) If we had listened to our inward witness, we would never have gone into business with certain people.

To define this inward witness in simple terms: As you are praying along a certain line and contemplating what to do, if there is a check in your spirit—a "something on the inside" that tells you not to do that—that is an inward witness. Sometimes you have to wait a while to get quiet enough to recognize it, however.

Someone once asked me, "How can I tell whether it is my own spirit or the Holy Spirit telling me to do something?"

I pointed out the Scripture that says, "The spirit of *man* is the candle of the Lord." God said He was going to use *your* spirit.

The man then replied, "But it may just be me that is wanting to do it."

"You ought to be able to tell whether it is the flesh—the outward man—who is wanting to do it, or the inward man," I said. "If it is the inward man, it is all right because the inward man is born anew and is a new creature. *'Old things are passed away; behold, all things are become new.'* The inward man has the nature and life of God in him. If you are Spirit-filled, the inward man has the Holy Spirit making His home in you. It isn't the inward man of a Christian who wants to do wrong; it's the outward man."

In John's epistle he talks about the seed of God abiding in this inward man, and he cannot sin. *"Whosoever is born of God doth not commit sin; for his seed remaineth in him: and he cannot sin, because he is born of God"* (1 John 3:9). This inward man has the nature and life of God in him because he is born of God.

Physically, we are born of our human parents, and we partake of their nature. We often hear people say, "He is just like his daddy," or "She looks just like her mother."

Spiritually, we are born of God and partake of His nature. *"Whereby are given unto us exceeding great and precious promises: that by these ye might be partakers of the divine nature . . . . "* (2 Peter 1:4). Peter also said we are born of the Word of God. *"Being born again, not of corruptible seed, but of incorruptible, by the word of God, which liveth and abideth for ever"* (1 Peter 1:23).

We are born of the Word of God; then, as we feed upon God's Word, we are made partakers of the divine nature. We know it is not the nature of God to do wrong. Therefore, if a person is really a Christian, a desire to do wrong is not in his spirit. (It is this outward man he struggles with.)

Looking at a Bible illustration of this inward witness, we read in Acts 27 the story of Paul on board a ship bound for Rome. *"Now when much time was spent, and when sailing was now dangerous, because the fast was now already past, Paul admonished them, And said unto them, Sirs, I perceive that this voyage will be with hurt and much damage not only of the lading and ship, but also of our lives"* (vv. 9,10).

Paul didn't say, "The Lord told me." It doesn't say that the Spirit of God said that to him. Paul said, "I *perceive.*" Who is the real "I"? It is the spirit-man, the man on the inside. Paul didn't perceive it mentally. He didn't perceive it physically. But in his spirit he had this witness.

A number of years ago a family went out to eat and while they were eating they suddenly sensed—they perceived—that they needed to rush home. They quickly finished their meal and rushed home. There they found that an emergency had arisen. They were able to do something about it because they perceived it in their spirits, just as Paul had.

Notice that Paul simply spoke what he perceived. He didn't threaten them if they didn't listen to him. No doubt they later wished that they had listened. I've had folks who didn't listen to me, but they later wished they had. You can't make people do things. God didn't tell us to force them. Some people issue dire warnings and threats if you don't listen to them and do what they say to do. These people have the wrong spirit. These things must be used in the spirit of love.

Paul states in First Corinthians 13 that the spiritual gifts can be used apart from love, and though they may bring blessing to some, they are not as effective as they should be. People would be so much more effective if they would act in love when they have something from God.

Then in Acts 27:20,21 we read, *"And when neither sun nor stars in many days appeared, and no small tempest lay on us, all hope that we should be saved was then taken away. But after long abstinence Paul stood forth in the midst of them and said, Sirs, ye should have hearkened unto me . . . ."* That was a bold statement.

Notice that Paul said, "You should have listened to me." He didn't say, "You should have listened to the Lord." He didn't say, "The Lord told me"; he said, "I perceive."

"Ye should have hearkened unto me, and not have loosed from Crete, and to have gained this harm and loss. And now I exhort you to be of good cheer: for there shall be no loss of any man's life among you, but of the ship . . . Wherefore, sirs, be of good cheer: for I believe God, that it shall be even as it was told me" (vv. 21, 22, 25).

Paul perceived danger, and if they had listened to him, they could have avoided shipwreck. But they didn't, so they lost all the merchandise and the ship. Yet Paul assured them that there would be no lives lost, *"for I believe God . . . "* and every man's life was saved.

A statement in Acts 13 will help us further in receiving guidance from God. *"Now there were in the church that was at Antioch certain prophets and teachers . . . As they ministered to the Lord, and fasted, the Holy Ghost said . . . . "* (Acts 13:1,2).

Notice under what conditions the Holy Spirit said something: *"As they ministered to the Lord, and fasted."* We don't have many services like that that I am aware of. Usually the preacher ministers to the people, not the Lord. Most of our church services are built on that principle. We are ministering to one another. But they ministered to the Lord. It was in that kind of atmosphere that the Holy Spirit spoke. It would be good for us today to have some services where we would minister to the Lord.

The Holy Spirit also leads us through what is known as the inward voice. When the Holy Spirit within you speaks, it will be a little more authoritative than the inward witness. When the voice of the Holy Spirit speaks, it is still an inward voice, but it is so real that you almost look around to see who spoke. At times when I have been praying and the Holy Spirit has spoken to me, I've looked behind me to see if someone was there. In my own mind, I knew that no one was there, but it seemed so real. He speaks to us in what seems to be an audible voice, though it may not be audible to anyone around us. Actually, we are not hearing it with the physical ear.

In the Old Testament we read where the young boy Samuel, who was just 12 years old at the time, heard a voice speaking to him in the nighttime. "Samuel," the voice called. He thought Eli was calling him, so he got up and went into Eli's room to ask what he wanted. Eli told him that he wasn't calling him. Samuel got back into bed. Then he heard it again—"Samuel." He got up again and went to Eli. He was sure Eli was calling. Then Eli realized that God was talking to Samuel, and he told him to answer the voice next time he heard it. When he did, the Lord began to speak to him. That wasn't an audible voice. It seemed audible to Samuel, but it wasn't. If it had been, Eli would have heard it, too, for he wasn't far from Samuel. It was God calling Samuel. (1 Samuel 3.)

Sometimes there is a similarity between the inward *witness* and the inward *voice*. Sometimes the witness is more distinct, and sometimes less distinct. The witness is simply a *check* or a *go-ahead* signal. The witness is sometimes like an inward buzzer to get our attention.

At other times the inward voice speaks to us. When we receive guidance through this inward voice, it will be in line with the Word. When the Spirit of God moves, He always moves in line with the Word. If it's not in line with the Word, it isn't the Spirit of God. The Bible is inspired by the Spirit, and if it is the same Spirit who is speaking to you, it is going to be in line with this Word.

We need to remember that the Bible says that there are many voices in this world. In my travels I meet people who claim to have heard some kind of a voice. The minute they start to tell me what they've heard, I know if they are right or wrong without judging them at all. I know the Word, so I know if it is in line with the Word or not.

I once met a lady who had been a wonderful Christian and a great blessing to the church. Of course, if the devil can mislead people, he can rob them of their Christian influence and testimony, and make them a curse instead of a blessing.

This woman told me about a revelation that she said the Lord had given to her. "I can't accept that," I told her, "because it's not in line with the Word."

"But I know the Lord spoke to me," she said. "I heard Him." Then she told about some kind of a vision she had had.

I repeated, "But it is not scriptural," and I began to quote Scriptures that contradicted what she was saying. Then I asked her, "Can you give me any Scripture to back up your revelation?"

She said, "Well, no, I can't."

I told her to open her Bible to a certain passage of Scripture. I knew that if she read that chapter, it would contradict everything she was saying. She read the verses I gave her. Then she shut the Bible and said, "Well, Bible or no Bible, I know God spoke to me and gave me this revelation. I'm going to stay with it."

I said, "God did not speak to you. If He had, He would have spoken to you in line with the Word. You don't have to take my word for it; you can read it for yourself."

She persisted, "Bible or no Bible, I'm going to stay with my revelation."

"All right," I finally replied, "you stay with yours, but I'm going to stay with God's."

There are some very dear people who have gotten off by following voices. There are many voices in the world. We are not to accept anything without examining it in the light of the Word.

God does communicate with us through our spirits, but it isn't a matter of listening to voices. It isn't a matter of praying to hear something. If He speaks to us, all right, but if He doesn't, we have His Word, and we can walk in the light of it.

3

GUIDANCE THROUGH VISIONS

GOD SOMETIMES leads us through visions. In the 10th chapter of Acts we read, *"There was a certain man in Caesarea called Cornelius ... A devout man, and one that feared God with all his house, which gave much alms to the people, and prayed to God alway. He saw in a vision evidently about the ninth hour of the day an angel of God coming in to him, and saying unto him, Cornelius .... "* (Acts 10:1-3).

Although Cornelius was a devout man, he was not a saved man. He was a Jewish proselyte. When Peter told the brethren in Jerusalem what had happened he said, *"And he* (Cornelius) *shewed us how he had seen an angel in his house, which stood and said unto him, Send men to Joppa, and call for Simon, whose surname is Peter; Who shall tell thee words, **whereby thou and all thy house shall be saved**"* (Acts 11:13,14).

The Scripture tells us that Cornelius saw an angel in a vision. Angels do have the ability, as God permits, to take upon themselves a form that can be seen with the natural eye. Paul said, *"Be not forgetful to entertain strangers: for thereby some have entertained angels unawares"* (Heb. 13:2). But the Scripture here calls Cornelius' experience a *vision*. If anyone else had been present, they probably would not have seen the angel.

There are three kinds of visions mentioned in the Scriptures.

The first is what is called *a spiritual vision*. You see with the eyes of your spirit; not with your physical eyes. When Paul saw the Lord in Acts 9, that was a spiritual vision. He didn't see Him with his physical eyes, because the Bible says, *"And when his eyes were opened, he saw no man"* (v. 8). He was blind. So when he heard the Lord speak to him, his eyes were shut, and when he opened them they were blind. Yet he said he saw the Lord. He was not seeing with his physical eyes; that was a spiritual vision.

The second type of vision is when one falls into *a trance*. Cornelius didn't fall into a trance, but the Scripture says that

Peter did. *"On the morrow, as they went on their journey, and drew nigh unto the city, Peter went up upon the housetop to pray about the sixth hour: And he became very hungry, and would have eaten: but while they made ready, he fell into a trance"* (Acts 10:9,10). When you fall into a trance, your physical senses are suspended. You don't know where you are. You don't know what is going on around you.

The third type of vision is what is called *an open vision*. That is where you actually see with your physical eyes open. Of all the visions I've had, only two of them have been open visions. I had my eyes wide open, and to me it was very real. In some of my other visions, I fell into a trance; others were spiritual visions.

Nonetheless, the Bible calls this appearance of the angel to Cornelius a vision. Then it tells us also that when Peter fell into a trance, he saw heaven open, and a certain vessel descending. In the 19th verse we read, *"While Peter thought on the vision . . . ."* Although this was a different type of vision, it was still a vision. He didn't know what it meant. Of course, Cornelius knew exactly what his vision meant, because the angel spoke to him telling him what to do: send men to Joppa to a certain house, and call for one Simon Peter, who would tell him how to be saved.

Notice that Cornelius did what the angel told him to do. The angel couldn't tell him how to be saved. God never ordained that angels should preach the gospel in the Church age; they can't. Men must preach the gospel. *"Go ye into all the world, and preach the gospel to every creature"* (Mark 16:15). All the angel could do was to tell him where to go to get someone who could tell him.

Second, notice that Peter's vision was symbolic. What he saw was a symbol of something; he didn't know immediately what it meant. He saw a great sheet let down from heaven on which were all kinds of four-footed beasts of the earth, wild beasts, creeping things, and fowls of the air. Then he heard a voice saying, *"Rise, Peter; kill, and eat"* (v. 13).

Peter was born again and filled with the Holy Spirit. But he had been brought up in the Jewish religion, and it is hard to get away from what you have been taught, whether it is right or wrong. Eating these things was against the beliefs of the Jewish

19

culture in which he was living, so he said, *"Not so, Lord; for I have never eaten any thing that is common or unclean"* (v. 14)

Jews were not supposed to eat certain foods. Some foods were clean, and some were unclean. This does not apply to us today, however. Paul taught this very clearly. Writing to Timothy he said, *"For every creature of God is good, and nothing to be refused, if it be received with thanksgiving: For it is sanctified by the word of God and prayer"* (1 Tim. 4:4,5).

"And the voice spake unto him again the second time, What God hath cleansed, that call not thou common. This was done thrice (in other words, he saw this and heard the voice three times): *and the vessel was received up again into heaven. Now while Peter doubted in himself what this vision which he had seen should mean . . . . "*

I think somehow on the inside of him Peter knew what the vision meant, but he doubted that it could *mean* that. Up until this time, the Church was strictly composed of Jewish believers. God was showing Peter in this vision that although the Jews considered the Gentiles unclean, God did not.

"While Peter thought on the vision, the Spirit said unto him . . . . " (v. 19) God spoke to him through this vision, but he still didn't know exactly what it meant. Yet, *"The Spirit said unto him* (referring to the Holy Spirit), *Behold, three men seek thee. Arise therefore, and get thee down, and go with them, doubting nothing: for I have sent them"* (vv. 19,20).

Another illustration showing God's guidance through supernatural means is found in Acts 8:26-29, *"And the angel of the Lord spake unto Philip, saying, Arise, and go toward the south unto the way that goeth down from Jerusalem unto Gaza, which is desert. And he arose and went: and, behold, a man of Ethiopia, an eunuch of great authority . . . had come to Jerusalem for to worship, Was returning, and sitting in his chariot read Esaias the prophet. Then the Spirit said unto Philip, Go near, and join thyself to this chariot."*

Let us pause to observe one thing: Some people admit that although God spoke to the apostles, such as Peter, such divine visitations were for the apostles only. Notice, however, that Philip was not an apostle. The best we can say about him is that he was an evangelist and a deacon. Yet the Lord spoke to him!

"The Spirit said unto Philip . . . . " It doesn't say *how* the Holy Spirit said it (whether it was audible), but we do know this wasn't just an inward witness. If that had been the case, it would have said the Spirit witnessed to Philip. But it doesn't say the Spirit *witnessed* to him; it says He *said* to him.

Notice something Jesus said about the Holy Spirit in John 16:13,14, *"Howbeit when he, the Spirit of truth, is come, he will guide you into all truth: for he shall not speak of himself; but whatsoever he shall hear, that shall he speak . . . . "* Jesus said that the Holy Spirit would speak, though not of Himself. This isn't referring to speaking in tongues. The Holy Spirit doesn't speak with tongues. The Holy Spirit gives you utterance, and *you* speak with tongues. *"And they were all filled with the Holy Ghost, and began to speak with other tongues, **as the Spirit gave them utterance**"* (Acts 2:4).

Jesus said, "He shall not speak of himself; but whatsoever he shall hear, that shall he speak." *Whatever the Holy Spirit hears God say, that is what He will speak to you. He is abiding in your spirit, and He can speak to your spirit.* I am convinced that the Holy Spirit spoke on the inside of Philip.

Notice also in the Scriptures concerning Peter's vision that the Spirit said something. *"While Peter thought on the vision, the Spirit said unto him, Behold, three men seek thee . . . . "* Again, it is my personal opinion (I do not know, because the Scripture only says the Spirit said it) that the Spirit didn't just witness to Peter's heart. If that had been the case, it would have said the Spirit witnessed to him. But it says, *"the Spirit said . . . . "*

We read about two other visions in Acts 9:10-12, *"And there was a certain disciple at Damascus, named Ananias; and to him said the Lord in a vision, Ananias. And he said, Behold, I am here, Lord. And the Lord said unto him, Arise, and go into the street which is called Straight, and enquire in the house of Judas for one called Saul, of Tarsus: for, behold, he prayeth, And hath seen in a vision a man named Ananias coming in, and putting his hand on him, that he might receive his sight."*

Ananias, like Philip, was only a disciple, not an apostle, yet God used him.

Of course, we don't have to wait for a vision before we do anything. God may give us a vision, or He may not, but we don't have to wait for one.

A number of years ago while I was holding a meeting in Dallas, a lady asked me to pray for her. "I always felt that God had something for me to do," she said. "I fasted and prayed three days, and the Lord told me to get out and do personal work."

I said, "Sister, if you had seen me, I could have saved you three days of fasting and praying. God wants all of us to be witnesses, and there are many different ways that we can witness. You don't have to pray three days and nights about that. Just go out and do it. Now, what is it you want me to pray about?"

"Well," she answered, "I want you to pray that I'll do it."

I said, "I'm not going to pray that you will do it. I'm going to pray that God will have mercy on your poor old lazy bones. You know what God wants you to do; now get out and do it."

That would be like a wife's saying, "I know I ought to get up and cook breakfast. I want you to pray for me that I'll do it." We will pray that the Lord will help you while you do it, but we won't pray that you will do it. You know that it is your job, so get after it. Trust Him as you go, and He will help you.

We don't have to wait on a vision to do something for God, but Ananias wouldn't have known a thing in the world about Saul, or that he was even praying, if God hadn't dealt with him in this way. The Lord appeared to Ananias in a vision and told him that there was a man in need. He wanted Ananias to go minister to him. Ananias answered, *"Lord, I have heard by many of this man, how much evil he hath done to thy saints at Jerusalem: And here he hath authority from the chief priests to bind all that call on thy name"* (vv. 13,14). In other words, Ananias was trying to say, "Are you sure, Lord, what you are doing? The last I heard of him he was putting believers in jail."

At the same time God also was dealing with Saul, who was a new convert. He had met Jesus on the road to Damascus, and he, too, had had a vision while he was praying. He saw a man named Ananias come and lay his hands on him that he might receive his sight.

An angel also may appear in a vision to us. A number of years ago there was a meeting of leaders of a Full Gospel denomination in which they discussed a fellow minister who claimed to have seen an angel in a vision. This angel was said to have directed him about his ministry, and he had set out to fulfill this ministry. Some of the ministers were quite concerned about him.

When it seemed that they were about ready to throw him out of the denomination for having seen an angel, one of the older ministers, who was an outstanding Bible teacher, said, "This comes at a very opportune moment. In the church that I pastor I asked the congregation to write on a piece of paper what subject they would like to hear discussed in our weekly Bible study. To my surprise, the majority of them said they had never heard any teaching on the subject of angels. I announced that I would teach on angels, thinking I would devote two or three services to the subject. But as I sat down with my Bible and began to study, I got so much material that it took me several weeks to teach it all. The thing that surprises me is *not* that this brother has seen an angel, but that more of us *haven't*."

Then he went on to give references from the Scriptures: how the angel of the Lord told Philip to go down by the way of Gaza, how the angel of God appeared to Paul on the ship, how the angel appeared to Cornelius, how the angel led Peter out of prison.

Then he said, "I don't mean that all of us should see angels, but that it should be a more common occurrence. I don't mean that it is going to be an everyday happening, or even that all of us would see an angel. But once in a while someone ought to. Since you have asked me to comment, I want to ask you this: If you take this away from us, have you anything better to put in its place?" They didn't, so they dismissed the subject instead of the minister who had seen the angel.

Let me say that although God does lead us through visions and other supernatural manifestations, I would encourage you not to seek a vision, because you might get out beyond God's Word to where the devil can deceive you. If we were to wait until we saw a vision or heard the audible voice of the Lord, we would miss these other things that are not as distinct, but are just as real.

We would prefer to have a more direct word of guidance, but we don't always get it. Don't try to manufacture it if it is not there. Just know that God always will guide you by some of these methods. Primarily it will be by the inward witness; then by the inward voice; then by these other ways as He wills, and not as you will. Don't seek these more spectacular ways of guidance. Nowhere does the Bible say that you are to seek these things. They just happen without your seeking them.

The Lord has appeared to me in visions seven or eight times, but on no occasion was I praying for them. I wasn't expecting them to happen when they did. Neither was I fasting at any time when Jesus appeared to me. That doesn't mean I don't believe in fasting, and that doesn't mean I don't fast, for I do. Some people leave the impression that if you would go on a long fast, you would receive some kind of manifestation. However, at no time was I on a fast when Jesus appeared to me. Visions always have come at a time when I least expected them.

I believe there is a reason for that. I think the Lord is trying to show us that we cannot do anything to "earn" visions. We can't do something to force His hand. Visions are not the result of works, but of grace.

We can learn some things about guidance in Acts 16. Paul and his company had been going about the regions of Galatia, and evidently they had wanted to go on into Asia. But they were *"forbidden by the Holy Ghost to preach the word in Asia"* (v. 6). When they tried to go to another place, *"the Spirit suffered them not."* Then in the nighttime a man appeared and said, *"Come over into Macedonia, and help us."* Then they *"endeavored to go into Macedonia, assuredly gathering that the Lord had called us."* They didn't have any direct word on it, but they *gathered* that this was what the Lord wanted them to do.

More than one was involved here, for the Scripture says "we." They didn't just let one person make the decision for them. They didn't even let Paul make the decision for them. *"We* assuredly gathered that the Lord had called *us* for to preach . . . . "* We read that the Spirit led, the Holy Ghost spoke, and the Spirit said. And the whole group that was present agreed that this was right.

Let us notice something else about the ministry and prophesying in Acts 15:32. *"And Judas and Silas, being prophets also themselves, exhorted the brethren with many* *words, and **confirmed** them."* They *confirmed* what the others already knew.

One final word of caution concerning prophecy and guidance: *I admonish folks to be very careful about personal prophecies.* As long as the gift stays in the realm of speaking to men *"to edification, and exhortation, and comfort,"* that is wonderful.

But many times someone who *prophesies* may see a *prophet* minister, and because he has a word of foreknowledge occasionally, he begins to think, "I prophesy, so I can do that." So he moves out of the place where he should be into this other realm of personal prophecy, and he is misled and misguided.

In many parts of the country, due to ignorance of the Scriptures and because people sometimes get carried away, there are those who are endeavoring to guide people's lives through spiritual gifts and prophecy. Then there are others who claim to be a prophet, or claim to minister along this line, who are leading people astray.

It is interesting to note that in Acts 21:10,11 Luke said, *"And as we tarried there many days, there came down from Judea a certain prophet, named Agabus. And when he was come unto us, he took Paul's girdle, and bound his own hands and feet, and said, Thus saith the Holy Ghost, So shall the Jews at Jerusalem bind the man that owneth this girdle, and shall deliver him into the hands of the Gentiles."* Notice that Agabus did not give Paul any guidance. He didn't tell him to go or not to go; he simply told him what the Holy Spirit said was going to come to pass.

I've known those who have listened to what someone else said by a so-called prophecy. I have seen some enter into marriage, and their lives have been ruined. Ministers have changed churches or entered into other ministries at the direction of some misguided prophecy, and they were never able to recover their loss. Businessmen have been terribly hurt by listening to someone who claimed to have a revelation from God. They invested their money and went bankrupt. I can't find any place in the New Testament that through a prophet's ministry anybody was told how to invest his money.

We thank God for the supernatural and for the inspirational gifts of the Spirit. But we must remember that the simple gift of prophecy (I'm not talking here about the ministry of the prophet) is speaking unto men to *"edification, and exhortation, and comfort"* (1 Cor. 14:3).

A denominational lady who had been attending prayer meetings in a home said to me recently, "Something is wrong with our prayer meetings. I don't know enough about it to understand what it is because I'm so new in it. We call it a prayer meeting, but we don't do any praying. All a lot of them do is spend two or three hours prophesying over one another. If any good has come of it, I don't know it. I've been filled with the Holy Spirit and have spoken with other tongues. I know it has been a great blessing to my life. But to me this sort of meeting is just a waste of time. All the prophecies I get are bad. One of them said my mother was going to die. She hasn't died yet. Another said my husband was going to leave me, but he hasn't left me yet."

This is not a true manifestation of the gift of prophecy, for it is not speaking unto men *"to edification, and exhortation, and comfort."* That didn't edify her or build her up; rather, it tore her down. It didn't comfort her a bit. It only worried her. It is certainly true that under certain conditions God may forewarn people in a number of ways about the death of a loved one to prepare their hearts. But He does it in a way that comforts them, not destroys them.

No matter who has a "word from the Lord" for you, if it doesn't confirm what you already have in your own spirit, don't accept it! We are all human and can make a mistake. A man isn't perfect just because he is a preacher. He could be wrong. That wouldn't mean he wasn't used of God. If you got in your car and weren't watching what you were doing, you might run up over a curb. That wouldn't mean that you couldn't drive just because you became a little negligent. A lot of times in spiritual things we aren't as keen as we should be. That is why the Bible tells us that these things have to be judged.

Someone once said to me, "An individual laid hands on me and said God had called me to the ministry. But if He did, I don't know it." I said, "If I were you, I'd forget it. If it doesn't confirm something you already have, then forget it."

Acts 13:2 says, *"As they ministered to the Lord, and fasted, the Holy Ghost said, Separate me Barnabas and Saul for the* *work whereunto I **have** called them."* God already had done it. Saul and Barnabas already had the calling. They already were in the ministry, but God was separating them to another ministry—to be apostles to the Gentiles.

The way God puts a man into an office is by giving him a gift for the task. It might be *confirmed* by prophecy sometimes, but the man is not *called* that way. All the prophesying in the world is not going to give a man the gift for that task. I've seen people upon whom someone laid hands and prophesied that they were to be an evangelist; yet they couldn't even give an adequate testimony, much less preach. If God has called you to do something, He will give you the necessary qualifications.

There is a very fine line between the real and the false; between reality and fanaticism. It is easy to step across that fine line, and then a lot of damage can be done. Because of misuse and excess, some people have become scared and have left these things alone altogether. They become dead and dry, and reject the miraculous. Then there are others who go to the other extreme and are ready to accept anything. They go off and follow what they call "the Spirit" and leave the Word. They end up in the ditch on the other side of the road. God doesn't want us to get in the ditch on either side of the road. He wants us to go right down the middle of the road.

In Acts 11:27,28 we read, *"And in these days came prophets from Jerusalem unto Antioch."* (There was more than one prophet evidently, because it says "prophets.") *"And there stood up one of them named Agabus, and signified by the spirit that there should be great dearth throughout all the world: which came to pass in the days of Claudius Caesar."*

This was more or less foretelling or prediction, but this was a prophet, not prophecy. It doesn't say Agabus prophesied; it says, *"he signified by the spirit."*

We read in Acts 16:6 of the ministry of Paul and Silas, *"Now when they had gone throughout Phrygia and the region of Galatia, and were forbidden of the Holy Ghost to preach the word in Asia."* Again, I want you to notice that a different expression is used when the Holy Ghost spoke directly to the individual. Regarding Peter, the Word says, *"The Holy Ghost said unto him."* Regarding Philip it says, *"the Spirit said unto Philip."* But here it says that the Spirit forbade them. Because both Paul and Silas were used in this manner, it causes me to believe that while they were praying, one of them spoke by prophecy.

It says they *"were forbidden of the Holy Ghost."* It doesn't say, "The Spirit told them not to go." They were *forbidden* of the Holy Ghost to preach in Asia. Didn't God want the Word to be preached in Asia? Yes, at the right time, for He said, *"Go ye into all the world, and preach the gospel to every creature"* (Mark 16:15).

Some preachers say, "It doesn't matter where you go to preach. God said to go into all the world, so I just go." But doesn't the Holy Spirit have anything to do with this? If we were all missionaries, there wouldn't be anyone to pastor the home church. If everyone wanted to go to India, who would go to Africa? We don't want to get away from the call of God. He may not want certain individuals to preach in certain countries. We must be open to do God's will.

4

GUIDANCE AND THE GIFT OF PROPHECY

I N STUDYING the gift of prophecy in connection with guidance, we need to understand that the ministry of the prophet and the gift of prophecy, while closely associated, are not the same. Many times the two are confused.

The fact that one prophesies does not make him a prophet. The Word of God plainly teaches that everyone should seek to prophesy. If prophesying made you a prophet, then it would seem that the Lord was saying that everyone ought to want to be a prophet. Yet Paul stated to the Corinthians that not all are prophets. *"Are all apostles? are all prophets?"* (1 Cor. 12:29). The answer is no, of course. Since all could not be prophets, he would not tell us to seek something we could not have. But all can prophesy.

The Bible teaches that the simple gift of prophecy is speaking unto men *"to edification, and exhortation, and comfort"* (1 Cor. 14:3). Prophecy is a supernatural utterance in a *known* tongue (your own tongue). Speaking with tongues is a supernatural utterance in an *unknown* tongue; that is, unknown to you. It may not be unknown to everybody.

Sometimes prophecy can be used in praying in your own language as well as in tongues. I have become so inspired to pray in English with the anointing of God's Spirit moving upon me that I have listened to myself pray for an hour. I knew it was coming out of me, but my mind didn't have a thing to do with it. I hadn't thought to pray about what I was praying about. It was prophecy—inspired utterance.

Sometimes when you are prophesying it will seem as if there are two of you. In a way, there are—the outward man and the inward man. This prophecy is coming out of the inward man, and the outward man listens. Sometimes when I am preaching, this anointing comes upon me and I hear myself saying things I hadn't planned to say. That is inspired utterance. Your mind doesn't have anything to do with it. It comes out of your spirit because of the Holy Spirit within you. This is a lower degree of the operation of the gift of prophecy.

As we have said, the fact that one prophesies doesn't make him a prophet. There is an office of the prophet. For a man to be a prophet, he stands in that office and uses that ministry.

The simple gift of prophecy is for speaking unto men *"to edification, and exhortation, and comfort,"* and should be used only in that area. In the simple gift of prophecy there is no foretelling; no prediction whatsoever.

However, there is foretelling and prediction in the ministry of the prophet because he has the revelation gifts in operation: the word of wisdom, the word of knowledge, and/or discerning of spirits.

Spiritual things, as well as natural things, can be misused. Some people say, "Well, if God is doing that, it has to be all right." But it isn't *exactly* God doing it. It is *men* doing it by the inspiration of the Spirit of God. Anything that man has anything to do with is not perfect. The Spirit of God is perfect, and the gifts of the Spirit in themselves are perfect, but they certainly are not always perfect in manifestation, because they are manifested through imperfect vessels. This is the reason that prophecies and tongues with interpretation need to be judged.

Paul said, *"Let the prophets speak two or three, and let the other judge"* (1 Cor. 14:29). They are to be judged according to the Bible. They aren't to be accepted without first judging them. *"If any thing be revealed to another that sitteth by . . . . "* (1 Cor. 14:30). Prophets have revelations. Others might occasionally, but prophets have a ministry along this line. God can give any Spirit-filled person a word of knowledge or a word of wisdom whenever He wants to for their own benefit, or to help somebody else.

The vocal gifts—tongues, interpretation of tongues, and prophecy—operate under the unction of the Spirit, but we initiate the operation of them. We *can* speak, or we can choose *not* to speak. We operate the gift. Some will say, "But God made me speak." However, the Bible plainly says, *"The spirits of the prophets are subject to the prophets"* (1 Cor. 14:32).

These gifts come through your spirit and are subject to your spirit. They shouldn't be operated without the unction of the

Spirit. Sometimes they are, and we have seen that they have not been a help to us. (This does not do away with the fact that they are real, however, just because they were in imperfect operation.)

Finally, let me say that when a child of God seeks to know His will for his life, God will make His perfect will completely clear to him by some means. Whether it be through a still small voice speaking to the heart of man, or through a supernatural manifestation of some kind, God will guide those whose hearts are open to Him in the pathway of peace.

For a clear, in-depth study along these lines, we suggest Kenneth E. Hagin's 144-page book, HOW YOU CAN BE LED BY THE SPIRIT OF GOD.